EMMANUEL JOSEPH

The Rhythm of the Mind, How Music, Brain Science, and Culture Shape Humanity

Contents

1

Chapter 1: The Universality of Music

Music transcends boundaries and brings people together from different cultures and backgrounds. Regardless of language or location, people everywhere create and enjoy music. From the rhythmic beats of African drums to the melodic tunes of European classical music, the universality of music is evident in every corner of the globe. This chapter explores the universality of music and its impact on human society throughout history. We delve into the ancient roots of music and its role in ritualistic and communal settings, highlighting how music has been a fundamental aspect of human life.

In ancient civilizations, music played a central role in rituals, ceremonies, and daily life. The ancient Egyptians, for example, used music in their religious practices to honor their gods and goddesses. Music was believed to have divine origins, and musicians were highly respected members of society. Similarly, in ancient Greece, music was an integral part of education and philosophy. The Greeks believed that music had the power to influence the soul and shape one's character.

Music's ability to bring people together is not limited to ancient times. In modern society, music continues to serve as a powerful tool for social cohesion. Concerts, festivals, and community events provide opportunities for individuals to come together and share in the collective experience of music. Whether it's a local band performing at a small venue or a world-renowned artist headlining a major music festival, the shared experience of music fosters a sense of unity and belonging.

The universality of music also extends to its ability to evoke emotions and memories. Music has the power to transport us to different times and places, triggering vivid recollections of past experiences. A particular song might remind us of a special moment with a loved one, or a specific melody might bring back memories of a significant event in our lives. This emotional connection to music is a testament to its profound impact on the human psyche.

2

Chapter 2: The Neuroscience of Music

Understanding how our brains process music is essential to comprehending its power. This chapter dives into the neuroscience behind music perception. It discusses the brain regions involved, the neural pathways activated by musical stimuli, and the effects of music on cognitive functions. From the auditory cortex to the emotional centers, we explore how music shapes our neurological responses.

The auditory cortex is the primary region of the brain responsible for processing sound. When we listen to music, sound waves enter our ears and are converted into electrical signals that travel to the auditory cortex. This region analyzes the various components of music, such as pitch, rhythm, and timbre. The brain's remarkable ability to differentiate and interpret these elements allows us to recognize melodies, harmonies, and complex musical structures.

However, music's influence on the brain extends beyond the auditory cortex. The limbic system, which regulates emotions, is also activated by musical stimuli. This connection between music and emotion is what makes music such a powerful and evocative art form. For instance, the amygdala, a key component of the limbic system, plays a crucial role in processing emotions associated with music. This is why a beautiful melody can bring us to tears, or an upbeat rhythm can fill us with joy.

Music also engages the brain's reward system, particularly the release of dopamine. Dopamine is a neurotransmitter associated with pleasure and reward. Listening to music that we enjoy stimulates the release of dopamine, creating a sense of euphoria. This neurochemical reaction explains why we often experience a "chill" or "goosebumps" when listening to our favorite songs.

Moreover, music's impact on cognitive functions is a fascinating area of study. Research has shown that musical training can enhance various cognitive skills, such as memory, attention, and problem-solving abilities. For example, learning to play an instrument requires the coordination of fine motor skills, auditory perception, and visual processing. This complex integration of sensory and motor functions strengthens neural connections and improves overall brain function.

In summary, the neuroscience of music reveals the intricate ways in which our brains process and respond to musical stimuli. The interaction between the auditory cortex, limbic system, and reward pathways highlights the profound impact of music on our emotions and cognitive abilities. As we continue to explore the neural mechanisms behind music, we gain a deeper appreciation for its extraordinary influence on the human mind.

3

Chapter 3: Music and Emotion

Music has a profound effect on our emotions, capable of eliciting a wide range of feelings from joy to sadness. This chapter examines the connection between music and emotion, exploring how different genres, rhythms, and melodies can evoke specific emotional responses. We discuss the psychological mechanisms behind this phenomenon and how music therapy is used to address emotional and mental health issues.

The connection between music and emotion is deeply rooted in human biology. When we listen to music, our brain releases neurotransmitters such as dopamine and serotonin, which play a crucial role in regulating mood and emotions. Upbeat music with fast tempos and major keys tends to evoke feelings of happiness and excitement, while slow, minor key compositions can induce feelings of melancholy or introspection.

Music therapy leverages the power of music to address emotional and mental health issues. This therapeutic approach involves using music to facilitate emotional expression, reduce stress, and improve overall well-being. Music therapists work with individuals of all ages, from children with developmental disorders to adults experiencing depression or anxiety. Through activities such as listening to music, playing instruments, and composing songs, music therapy helps individuals process their emotions and achieve a sense of emotional balance.

In addition to its therapeutic benefits, music also plays a significant role in everyday emotional experiences. People often turn to music to enhance their moods, cope with difficult situations, and connect with their inner selves. Whether it's a soothing melody to unwind after a long day or an energetic beat to motivate a workout, music serves as a powerful tool for emotional regulation and self-expression.

4

Chapter 4: Cultural Influences on Music

Culture plays a significant role in shaping the music we create and enjoy. This chapter explores the diverse musical traditions from around the world, examining how cultural contexts influence musical styles, instruments, and practices. We delve into the intersection of music and cultural identity, highlighting the ways in which music reflects and reinforces cultural values and norms.

Different cultures have developed unique musical traditions that reflect their histories, beliefs, and social structures. For example, traditional African music is characterized by complex rhythms and percussion instruments, often used in communal celebrations and rituals. In contrast, classical music from Western Europe is known for its emphasis on harmony, melody, and the use of orchestral instruments.

Music also serves as a means of preserving and transmitting cultural heritage. Folk songs, traditional dances, and ceremonial music are passed down through generations, keeping cultural identities alive. In many indigenous communities, music is an integral part of storytelling and oral history, conveying important cultural narratives and values.

The influence of culture on music is not limited to traditional forms. Contemporary music genres such as hip-hop, reggae, and K-pop have emerged from specific cultural contexts and have gained global popularity. These genres often address social and political issues, reflecting the experiences and aspirations of the communities that created them. Through music, cultural expressions are shared and appreciated across borders, fostering cross-cultural understanding and appreciation.

5

Chapter 5: The Role of Music in Social Cohesion

Music has the power to unite people and foster social bonds. This chapter discusses the role of music in promoting social cohesion, examining how communal music-making and shared musical experiences strengthen group identity and solidarity. We explore examples from various cultures where music is used in ceremonies, festivals, and social movements to bring people together.

In many societies, music is an essential part of communal activities and celebrations. Festivals, religious ceremonies, and public gatherings often feature music as a central element, creating a sense of collective identity and belonging. For example, in Brazil, the annual Carnival celebration involves vibrant music, dance, and parades, bringing people from diverse backgrounds together in a joyful expression of cultural unity.

Music also plays a crucial role in social movements and activism. Throughout history, protest songs and anthems have been used to mobilize communities, express dissent, and inspire change. Songs like "We Shall Overcome" during the Civil Rights Movement and "Blowin' in the Wind" during the anti-war protests of the 1960s became rallying cries for social justice and political activism. These songs provided a sense of solidarity and hope, galvanizing individuals to come together and fight for a common cause.

Moreover, communal music-making activities, such as choir singing, drumming circles, and jam sessions, foster social connections and collaboration. Participating in group music activities encourages teamwork, communication, and empathy, strengthening the bonds between individuals. The shared experience of creating and enjoying music fosters a sense of community and mutual support, contributing to social cohesion and harmony.

6

Chapter 6: Music and Cognitive Development

The impact of music on cognitive development is a fascinating area of study. This chapter explores the benefits of musical training and exposure on brain development, particularly in children. We discuss how learning to play an instrument, engage in musical activities, and listen to music can enhance cognitive skills such as memory, attention, and language.

Musical training involves the integration of auditory, motor, and visual skills, which stimulates various regions of the brain. Research has shown that children who learn to play an instrument tend to perform better in tasks that require auditory discrimination, such as distinguishing between different pitches and rhythms. These enhanced auditory skills can also translate to improved language abilities, as both music and language share common neural pathways.

Furthermore, learning to play an instrument requires the coordination of fine motor skills, which strengthens the brain's motor regions. This enhanced motor control can have positive effects on other activities that involve precise movements, such as writing and sports. The discipline and practice required for musical training also foster important executive functions, such as sustained attention, impulse control, and goal-setting.

Listening to music can also have cognitive benefits. For example, exposure to classical music has been associated with improved spatial reasoning skills, a phenomenon known as the "Mozart effect." While the exact mechanisms behind this effect are still debated, it is clear that engaging with music can stimulate cognitive processes and enhance brain plasticity.

In summary, music plays a significant role in cognitive development, particularly in children. The integration of auditory, motor, and visual skills in musical training enhances various cognitive abilities, contributing to overall brain development. As we continue to uncover the connections between music and cognition, we gain a deeper appreciation for the role of music in shaping young minds.

7

Chapter 7: The Healing Power of Music

Music has therapeutic properties that can promote healing and well-being. This chapter delves into the field of music therapy, exploring how music is used to address physical, emotional, and psychological health issues. We discuss the evidence-based practices in music therapy and share real-life case studies demonstrating its effectiveness in various clinical settings.

Music therapy involves the use of music to achieve therapeutic goals, such as reducing anxiety, improving mood, and enhancing physical rehabilitation. Music therapists work with individuals of all ages and backgrounds, tailoring interventions to meet the specific needs of each client. Activities may include listening to music, singing, playing instruments, and composing songs.

One of the key benefits of music therapy is its ability to evoke emotional responses and facilitate emotional expression. For individuals who struggle to articulate their feelings verbally, music provides a nonverbal outlet for emotional release. Music therapy has been shown to be particularly effective in addressing issues such as depression, anxiety, and trauma.

In addition to its emotional benefits, music therapy can also promote physical healing. For example, rhythmic auditory stimulation has been used to improve gait and motor function in individuals with neurological disorders, such as Parkinson's disease and stroke. The rhythmic nature of music helps to synchronize movement, facilitating smoother and more coordinated motor actions.

Real-life case studies highlight the transformative power of music therapy. In one example, a young boy with autism who had difficulty communicating found his voice through music. By engaging in music therapy sessions, he was able to improve his social interactions and express himself more effectively. Similarly, a stroke survivor who had lost the ability to speak regained her speech through melodic intonation therapy, a music-based intervention that uses singing to stimulate language production.

The healing power of music extends to various clinical settings, including hospitals, rehabilitation centers, and mental health facilities. As we continue to explore the therapeutic potential of music, it is clear that music therapy offers a valuable and effective approach to promoting health and well-being.

8

Chapter 8: The Influence of Music on Behavior

Music can influence human behavior in subtle yet profound ways. This chapter examines how different types of music affect our actions, decisions, and social interactions. We explore the role of music in shaping consumer behavior, its use in marketing, and how certain genres can inspire or deter specific behaviors in different contexts.

Music's influence on behavior can be observed in everyday situations, such as shopping or dining. Retailers often use background music to create a specific atmosphere that encourages spending. For example, upbeat and lively music can create a sense of urgency and excitement, prompting customers to make impulsive purchases. In contrast, slow and calming music can create a relaxed environment, encouraging customers to spend more time in the store and explore its offerings.

The use of music in marketing is another powerful tool for influencing behavior. Advertisers carefully select music that resonates with their target audience, creating memorable and emotionally engaging advertisements. A catchy jingle or a well-chosen song can leave a lasting impression, making consumers more likely to recall and purchase a product.

Music can also inspire specific behaviors in different contexts. For example, energetic and fast-paced music is often used in fitness classes to motivate participants and enhance their performance. In contrast, soothing and ambient music is used in relaxation and meditation practices to promote a sense of calm and mindfulness.

Furthermore, certain genres of music can influence social interactions and group dynamics. For example, heavy metal and punk rock are often associated with rebellious and anti-establishment attitudes, while classical music is associated with sophistication and intellectualism. These associations can shape how individuals perceive and interact with each other based on their musical preferences.

In summary, music has a profound influence on human behavior, affecting our actions, decisions, and social interactions. By understanding the ways in which music shapes behavior, we can harness its power to create positive and meaningful experiences in various aspects of life.

9

Chapter 9: Music in Education

Incorporating music into educational settings can have significant benefits for students. This chapter discusses the role of music in education, highlighting how it can enhance learning experiences and academic performance. We examine various pedagogical approaches that integrate music into the curriculum and the positive impact it has on student engagement and achievement.

Music education provides students with opportunities to develop a wide range of skills, including creativity, critical thinking, and collaboration. Learning to play an instrument, for example, requires discipline, practice, and perseverance, fostering important executive functions. Participating in ensemble performances, such as school bands or choirs, encourages teamwork and communication, helping students develop social skills.

Integrating music into other subjects can also enhance academic performance. For example, using songs to teach mathematical concepts can make learning more engaging and enjoyable. Rhythmic patterns and musical notation can help students understand abstract mathematical principles, such as fractions and ratios. Similarly, incorporating music into language arts lessons can improve literacy skills by enhancing phonological awareness and vocabulary acquisition.

Research has shown that students who participate in music education tend to perform better academically. For example, a study found that students who received music instruction scored higher on standardized tests in reading and mathematics compared to their peers who did not receive music instruction. The cognitive and emotional benefits of music education contribute to improved academic outcomes and overall student well-being.

Moreover, music education provides a platform for self-expression and creativity. Through composing and improvising, students can explore their own musical ideas and develop their unique artistic voices. This creative outlet fosters a sense of identity and self-confidence, empowering students to express themselves and share their perspectives.

In summary, music education plays a vital role in enhancing learning experiences and academic performance. By integrating music into the curriculum, educators can create a rich and dynamic learning environment that supports the holistic development of students.

10

Chapter 10: Music and Creativity

Music is a powerful catalyst for creativity and innovation. This chapter explores the relationship between music and creativity, discussing how musical activities can stimulate imaginative thinking and problem-solving abilities. We delve into the ways in which musicians and composers draw inspiration from different sources and how music can foster a creative mindset.

The act of creating music requires a blend of technical skill and imaginative thought. Composers and songwriters often draw inspiration from a variety of sources, such as personal experiences, emotions, nature, literature, and other art forms. By weaving these elements together, they create original and expressive works that resonate with audiences. The creative process of composing music involves experimentation, improvisation, and iteration, allowing musicians to explore new ideas and push the boundaries of their artistic expression.

Engaging in musical activities can also enhance creative thinking in other domains. For example, improvisation exercises, where musicians spontaneously create music in response to a given stimulus, encourage flexible thinking and adaptability. These skills can be applied to problem-solving scenarios in various fields, such as science, technology, and business. The ability to think outside the box and approach challenges from multiple perspectives is a hallmark of creativity, and music provides a rich platform for developing these cognitive abilities.

Moreover, music can serve as a source of inspiration for other creative endeavors. Many artists, writers, and designers find that listening to music can stimulate their imagination and help them generate new ideas. The emotional and sensory experiences elicited by music can spark creative thoughts and provide a unique perspective on their work. For example, a painter might use the mood and rhythm of a piece of music to influence the colors and brushstrokes in their artwork, creating a multisensory connection between music and visual art.

In summary, music is a powerful catalyst for creativity and innovation. The process of creating and engaging with music stimulates imaginative thinking and problem-solving abilities, fostering a creative mindset. By exploring the connections between music and other creative domains, we gain a deeper appreciation for the role of music in inspiring and nurturing human creativity.

11

Chapter 11: The Future of Music

The future of music is shaped by technological advancements and evolving cultural trends. This chapter examines the impact of digital technology on music creation, distribution, and consumption. We discuss the rise of new musical genres, the role of artificial intelligence in music production, and the challenges and opportunities presented by the digital age.

The advent of digital technology has revolutionized the music industry, transforming the way music is created and shared. Digital audio workstations (DAWs) and music production software have made it possible for musicians to produce high-quality recordings from their home studios. This democratization of music production has given rise to a diverse array of independent artists and genres, expanding the musical landscape.

Streaming platforms and social media have also changed the way we access and consume music. Listeners can now discover and enjoy a vast library of music from around the world with just a few clicks. This increased accessibility has led to the rise of niche genres and subcultures, as well as the global spread of musical trends. The ability to share and promote music online has provided artists with new opportunities to reach audiences and build their fanbase.

Artificial intelligence (AI) is playing an increasingly significant role in music production and composition. AI algorithms can analyze vast amounts of musical data to generate original compositions, suggest chord progressions, and enhance audio quality. AI-powered tools are also being used to personalize music recommendations, helping listeners discover new artists and songs that align with their preferences. While AI is unlikely to replace human creativity, it offers valuable tools that can augment the creative process and push the boundaries of musical innovation.

However, the digital age also presents challenges for the music industry. Issues such as copyright infringement, data privacy, and fair compensation for artists remain ongoing concerns. The rise of streaming services has shifted the economic model of the music industry, with many artists advocating for more equitable revenue-sharing practices. As technology continues to evolve, it is essential to address these challenges and create a sustainable and inclusive environment for musicians and listeners alike.

In conclusion, the future of music is shaped by technological advancements and cultural trends. Digital technology has transformed the way music is created, distributed, and consumed, offering new opportunities and challenges. As we navigate the digital age, we must embrace innovation while addressing the ethical and economic implications of these changes.

12

Chapter 12: The Enduring Power of Music

Despite the changes in how music is created and experienced, its fundamental power remains unchanged. This chapter reflects on the enduring significance of music in human life, emphasizing its role in shaping our minds, emotions, and cultures. We conclude by celebrating the timeless and universal nature of music and its profound influence on humanity.

Music has been an integral part of human existence for millennia, transcending time and space. Its ability to evoke emotions, tell stories, and bring people together is a testament to its enduring power. Whether it is a traditional folk song passed down through generations or a contemporary pop hit that resonates with millions, music has the capacity to touch our hearts and souls in profound ways.

The universal nature of music allows it to bridge cultural divides and foster cross-cultural understanding. In an increasingly interconnected world, music serves as a common language that can unite people from diverse backgrounds. Collaborative musical projects that bring together artists from different cultures and genres showcase the beauty of diversity and the potential for creative synergy.

Moreover, music's impact on our minds and emotions highlights its importance in our daily lives. From providing solace during difficult times to enhancing joyous celebrations, music accompanies us through the full spectrum of human experiences. Its therapeutic properties promote healing and well-being, offering comfort and support when words alone are insufficient.

As we reflect on the role of music in human life, it is clear that its significance extends beyond mere entertainment. Music is a powerful force that shapes our identities, enriches our cultures, and connects us to one another. Its timeless and universal nature ensures that it will continue to inspire and uplift humanity for generations to come.

In conclusion, music's enduring power lies in its ability to evoke emotions, tell stories, and bring people together. Its universal and timeless nature ensures its continued relevance and influence in our lives. As we celebrate the profound impact of music on humanity, we are reminded of its unique ability to shape our minds, emotions, and cultures in meaningful and lasting ways.

13

Chapter 13: Music and Technology

The relationship between music and technology has evolved significantly over the years. This chapter explores how technological advancements have influenced the creation, production, and distribution of music. From the invention of musical instruments to the rise of digital audio workstations and streaming platforms, we examine how technology has transformed the music industry and shaped the way we experience music.

The invention of musical instruments, such as the piano, electric guitar, and synthesizer, has expanded the possibilities for musical expression. These innovations have allowed musicians to explore new sounds, genres, and techniques, pushing the boundaries of creativity. Additionally, recording technology, from analog tape to digital audio, has revolutionized the way music is produced and shared with audiences.

The advent of digital technology has further democratized music production and distribution. With the rise of digital audio workstations (DAWs) and music production software, aspiring musicians can now create high-quality recordings from the comfort of their homes. Online platforms, such as YouTube, SoundCloud, and Spotify, have made it easier for independent artists to share their music with a global audience and build their fanbase.

Furthermore, advancements in artificial intelligence (AI) and machine learning are transforming the music industry. AI-powered tools can assist in music composition, analysis, and recommendation, offering new possibilities for creativity and personalization. As technology continues to evolve, it will undoubtedly shape the future of music in exciting and unforeseen ways.

14

Chapter 14: Music and Identity

Music plays a crucial role in shaping individual and collective identities. This chapter explores how music reflects and reinforces personal and cultural identities, examining the ways in which musical preferences, practices, and performances contribute to our sense of self and belonging.

On an individual level, musical preferences can be a powerful expression of identity. The genres, artists, and songs we choose to listen to often reflect our personality, values, and experiences. For many people, music serves as a form of self-expression, providing a means to articulate their emotions, beliefs, and aspirations. Whether it's the rebellious spirit of punk rock, the introspective nature of indie folk, or the uplifting energy of pop, music allows individuals to connect with their inner selves and communicate their identity to the world.

Music also plays a significant role in shaping cultural identities. Different musical traditions and genres are often closely tied to specific cultural groups and communities. For example, reggae music is deeply rooted in Jamaican culture, reflecting the island's history, struggles, and triumphs. Similarly, flamenco music is an essential part of Spanish culture, embodying the passion and spirit of the Andalusian people. By preserving and promoting these musical traditions, communities can maintain their cultural heritage and foster a sense of pride and belonging.

Moreover, music can serve as a unifying force, bringing people together and creating a shared sense of identity. National anthems, protest songs, and cultural festivals are examples of how music can symbolize collective values, aspirations, and experiences. Through these shared musical experiences, individuals can connect with others who share their cultural background or ideological beliefs, strengthening social bonds and fostering a sense of community.

15

Chapter 15: Music and Spirituality

Music has long been associated with spirituality and religious practices. This chapter explores the role of music in spiritual and religious contexts, examining how it is used to facilitate worship, meditation, and transcendental experiences. We discuss the ways in which music can evoke a sense of the divine and provide a pathway to spiritual enlightenment.

Throughout history, music has been an integral part of religious rituals and ceremonies. In many cultures, sacred music is believed to have the power to connect believers with the divine, facilitate prayer, and create a sense of reverence and awe. For example, Gregorian chants in the Christian tradition are used to create a meditative and contemplative atmosphere, while Sufi music in Islam is employed to induce a state of spiritual ecstasy and connection with God.

Music's ability to evoke emotions and alter consciousness makes it a powerful tool for spiritual practices. Meditative and ambient music, with its soothing and repetitive patterns, can help individuals achieve a state of deep relaxation and mindfulness. Similarly, rhythmic drumming and chanting are often used in shamanic and indigenous rituals to facilitate trance states and spiritual journeys.

Moreover, music can provide a sense of transcendence and unity, allowing individuals to connect with something greater than themselves. Whether through communal singing, devotional hymns, or mystical compositions, music has the power to uplift the soul and inspire spiritual growth. By exploring the intersection of music and spirituality, we gain a deeper understanding of the profound ways in which music enriches our spiritual lives.

In "**The Rhythm of the Mind: How Music, Brain Science, and Culture Shape Humanity**," embark on a captivating journey that explores the profound influence of music on our brains, emotions, and cultures. This book delves into the universality of music, tracing its ancient roots and highlighting its role in bringing people together across different cultures and backgrounds.

Uncover the fascinating neuroscience behind music perception and learn how our brains process and respond to musical stimuli, engaging regions such as the auditory cortex and limbic system. Discover the powerful connection between music and emotion, and explore how music therapy is used to address emotional and mental health issues.

Dive into the diverse musical traditions from around the world and understand how culture shapes the music we create and enjoy. Learn about the role of music in promoting social cohesion, enhancing cognitive development, and fostering creativity and innovation.

With chapters on the healing power of music, the influence of music on behavior, and the integration of music into education, this book provides a comprehensive overview of the multifaceted impact of music on human life. Explore the intersection of music and spirituality, and reflect on the enduring significance of music in shaping our identities and enriching our cultures.

"The Rhythm of the Mind" celebrates the timeless and universal nature of music and its profound influence on humanity. Whether you're a music enthusiast, a curious reader, or a professional in the field, this book offers valuable insights into the transformative power of music and its essential role in our lives.